DEMCO

Tarantulas

by Helen Frost

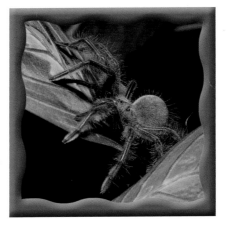

Consulting Editor: Gail Saunders-Smith, Ph.D.

Consultant: Rhys A. Brigida, President
American Tarantula Society

Pebble Books

an imprint of Capstone Press
Mankato, Minnesota

Pebble Books are published by Capstone Press
151 Good Counsel Drive, P.O. Box 669, Mankato, Minnesota 56002
http://www.capstone-press.com

1 2 3 4 5 6 07 06 05 04 03 02

Library of Congress Cataloging-in-Publication Data
Frost, Helen, 1949–
   Tarantulas/by Helen Frost
   p. cm.—(Rain forest animals)
   Includes bibliographical references (p. 23) and index.
   Summary: Simple text and photographs from the rain forest present the
characteristics and behavior of tarantulas.
   ISBN 0-7368-1195-8
   1. Tarantulas—Juvenile literature. [1. Tarantulas. 2. Spiders.] I. Title. II. Series.
QL458.42.T5 F76 2002
595.4′4—dc21
                                                            2001003106

Note to Parents and Teachers

The Rain Forest Animals series supports national science
standards related to life science. This book describes and
illustrates tarantulas living in the rain forest. The labeled
photographs support early readers in understanding the text.
Some labels provide the common name for the tarantula. Other
labels use the scientific name for the tarantula. The repetition of
words and phrases helps early readers learn new words. This
book also introduces early readers to subject-specific vocabulary
words, which are defined in the Words to Know section. Early
readers may need assistance to read some words and to use the
Table of Contents, Words to Know, Read More, Internet Sites,
and Index/Word List sections of the book.

Table of Contents

4

Tarantulas are hairy spiders. They are some of the largest spiders in the world.

antilles pinktoe tarantula

Indian ornamental tarantula

Pamphobeteus specie.

Tarantulas can
be many colors.

Tarantulas have eight legs. They have two sharp fangs that inject venom.

cobalt blue tarantula

places tarantulas live

Many tarantulas live
in tropical rain forests
and other warm places.

emergent layer

canopy layer

understory layer

forest floor

12

Tarantulas creep across
the canopy layer
and the forest floor.

14

Some tarantulas
dig burrows
in the ground.
Other tarantulas
spin webs in trees.

Cyriopagopus species

Tarantulas hunt prey at night. They catch frogs, moths, and other tarantulas.

Peruvian pinktoe tarantula eating a frog

Tarantulas bite their prey. The venom from their fangs kills the prey.

Brazilian fire-red tarantula eating a cockroach

Tarantulas rest
in their burrows
during the day.

Cyriopagopus species

Words to Know

burrow—a tunnel or hole that an animal digs in the ground

canopy—the layer of treetops that forms a covering over a rain forest

fang—a body part that looks like a long, pointed tooth; tarantula fangs are hollow.

forest floor—the bottom part of the rain forest; almost no sunlight reaches the forest floor.

inject—to put into; tarantulas use their fangs to inject venom into prey.

tropical rain forest—a dense area of trees where rain falls almost every day

venom—a substance produced by some spiders and snakes; tarantula venom can kill prey; it usually is not harmful to people.

web—a fine net of silky threads; some tarantulas make strong, tube-shaped webs; other tarantulas do not make webs.

Read More

McGinty, Alice B. *Tarantula.* The Library of Spiders. New York: PowerKids Press, 2002.

Murray, Peter. *Tarantulas.* Chanhassen, Minn.: Child's World, 2001.

Steele, Christy. *Tarantulas.* Animals of the Rain Forest. Austin, Texas: Raintree Steck-Vaughn, 2001.

Internet Sites

American Tarantula Society
http://www.atshq.org

Brain Pop: Rain Forest Movie
http://www.brainpop.com/science/ecology/rainforest/index.weml

Rain Forest Animals
http://www.enchantedlearning.com/subjects/rainforest

Index/Word List

Word Count: 97
Early-Intervention Level: 13

Editorial Credits
Sarah Lynn Schuette, editor; Jennifer Schonborn, production designer and interior
    illustrator; Linda Clavel, cover designer; Heidi Meyer, cover designer; Kia Bielke,
    interior illustrator; Kimberly Danger and Mary Englar, photo researchers

Photo Credits
Digital Vision, 10
James E. Gerholdt, 1
James P. Rowan, cover
Rick C. West, 6 (top and bottom), 8, 14, 16, 20
Robert and Linda Mitchell, 4, 18

Pebble Books thanks Dr. Robert Gale Breene III from the American Tarantula Society
for also reviewing this book.

24